BIBLE BLOSSOM
STORYBOOK

Bible Blossom Storybook: The Unfolding Story of God

© 2019. The Urban Ministry Institute. All Rights Reserved. Copying, redistribution, and/or sale of these materials, or any unauthorized transmission, except as may be expressly permitted by the 1976 Copyright Act or in writing from the publisher is prohibited. Requests for permission should be addressed in writing to:

The Urban Ministry Institute
3701 East 13th Street North
Wichita, KS 67208

ISBN: 978-1-62932-319-0

Published by TUMI Press
A division of World Impact, Inc.

The Urban Ministry Institute is a ministry of World Impact, Inc.

All Scripture quotations, unless otherwise noted, are from The Holy Bible, English Standard Version, © 2001 by Crossway Bible, a division of Good News Publishers. Used by permission. All Rights Reserved.

BIBLE BLOSSOM

STORYBOOK

The Unfolding Story of God

written by
REV. RYAN CARTER AND REV. DR. DON L. DAVIS

with illustrations by
TIM LADWIG

TUMI Press • 3701 East 13th Street North • Wichita, Kansas 67208

Prologue

From the Beginning to the Fullness of Time

Creation and the Fall

In eternity past, God determined to send his Son to save a people from death

1 Peter 1.18-21

1

In the beginning God created the heavens and the earth

Genesis 1.1-2.3

2

The first human pair in the Garden of Eden
Genesis 2.4-25

3

The serpent tempts the woman
Genesis 3.1-7

This symbol represents a type of Christ in the Old Testament, foreshadowing some aspect of his person or work which Jesus of Nazareth would fulfill at his appearing. Jesus is the anti-type (i.e., the one to whom the type points and anticipates) of many of the objects, ceremonies, episodes, people, and events within the Old Testament. Truly, Jesus of Nazareth is the theme of the Bible (John 5.39-40; Luke 24.27, 44-48).

God promises a Savior
Genesis 3.8-21

4

5

Adam and Eve are banished from the Garden

Genesis 3.22-24

6

Cain kills his brother, Abel

Genesis 4.1-16

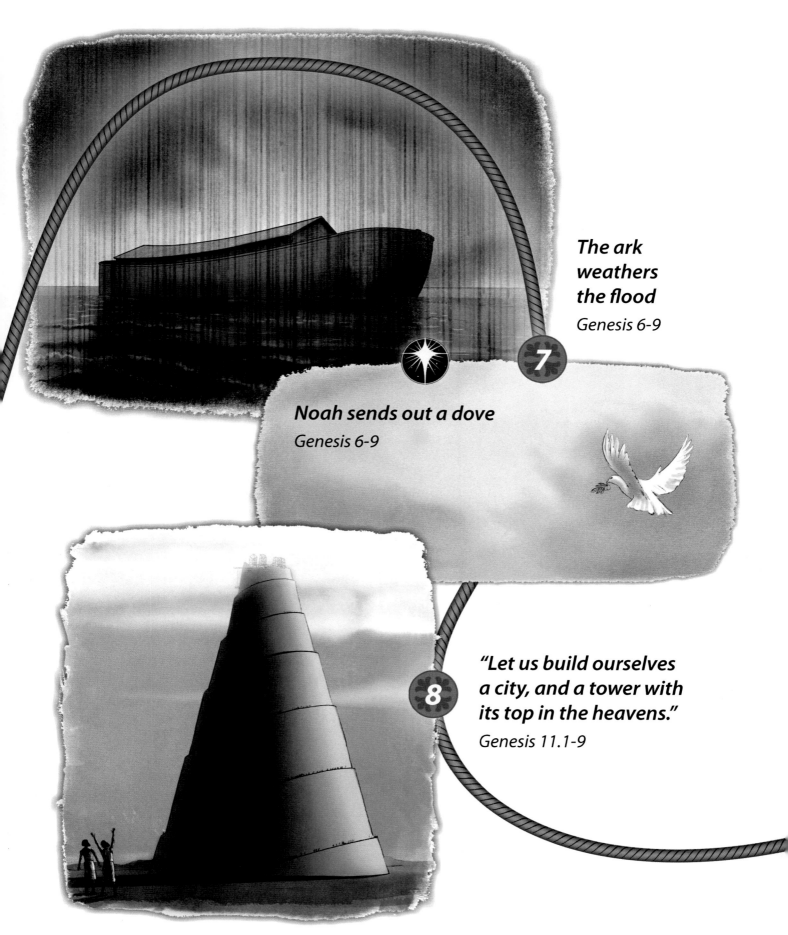

The ark weathers the flood

Genesis 6-9

7

Noah sends out a dove

Genesis 6-9

8

"Let us build ourselves a city, and a tower with its top in the heavens."

Genesis 11.1-9

The Promise and the Patriarchs

9

God makes a covenant with Abraham

Genesis 12, 15

10

*Melchizedek
blesses Abraham*
Genesis 14.17-24

Lot flees Sodom with his family

Genesis 19

11

Abraham prepares to sacrifice Isaac
Genesis 22.1-19

12

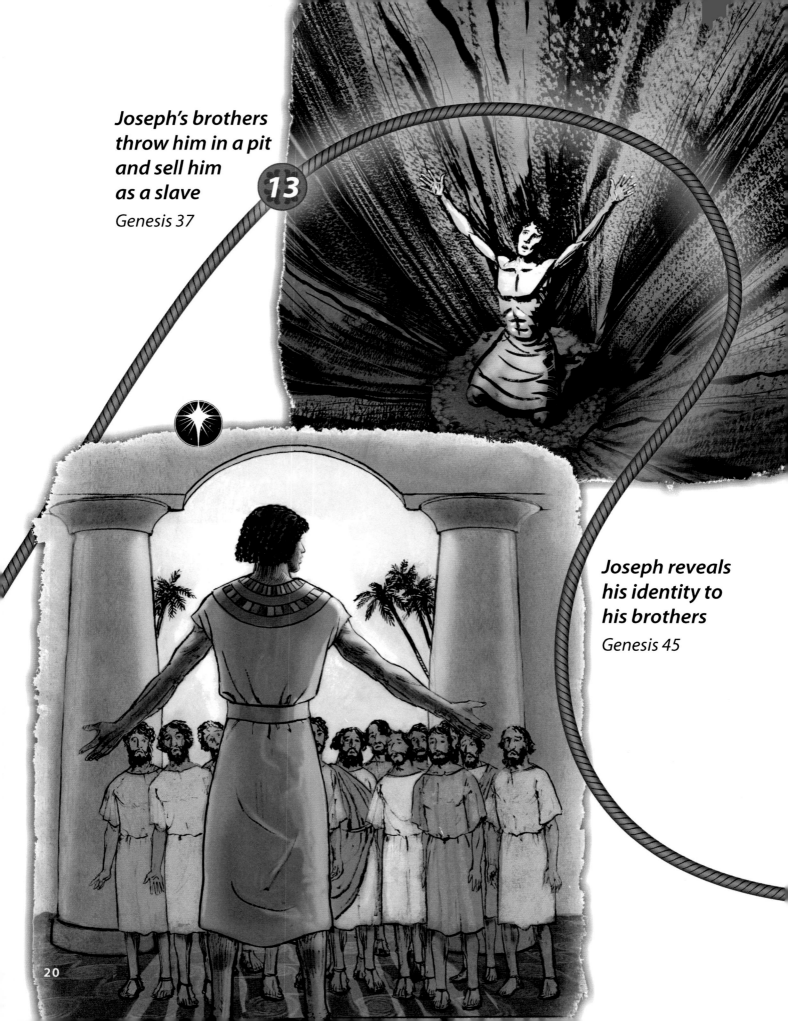

Joseph's brothers throw him in a pit and sell him as a slave

Genesis 37

13

Joseph reveals his identity to his brothers

Genesis 45

Deliverance from Egypt

14 Baby Moses in the Nile River
Exodus 1-2

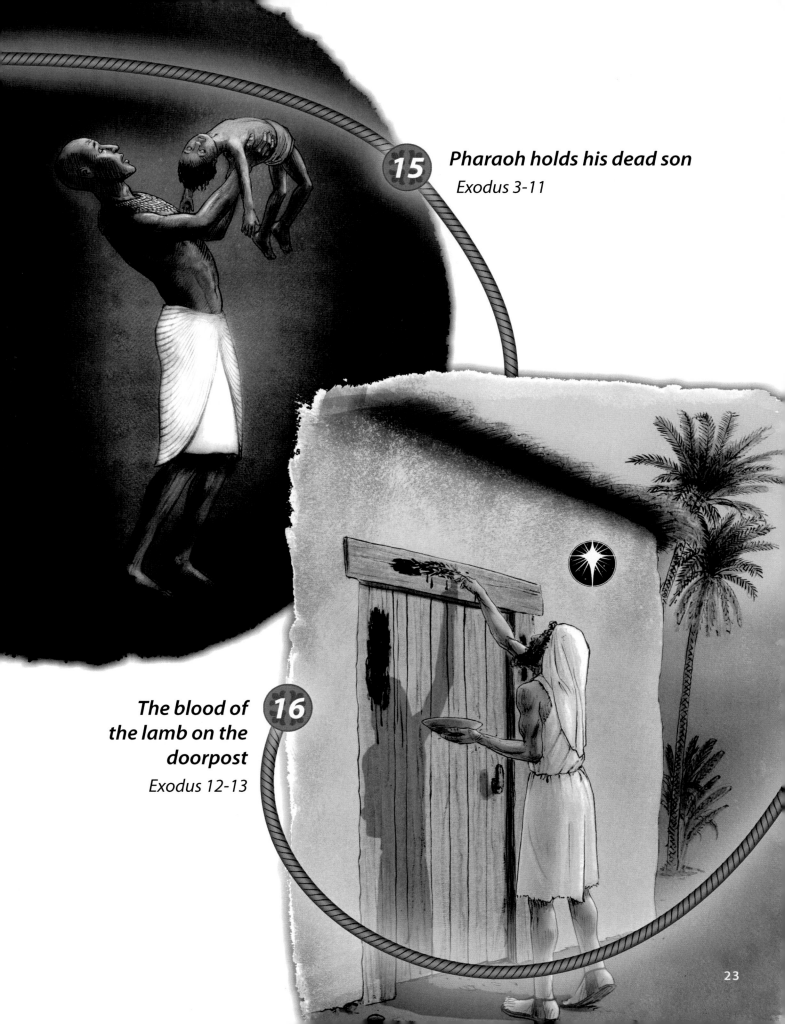

15 **Pharaoh holds his dead son**
Exodus 3-11

The blood of the lamb on the doorpost **16**
Exodus 12-13

23

17 Moses leads Israel through the Red Sea
Exodus 14-15

The Tabernacle of the Lord **18**
Exodus 40

24

From Egypt to Canaan

19

The spies return from Canaan

Numbers 13.1-14.10

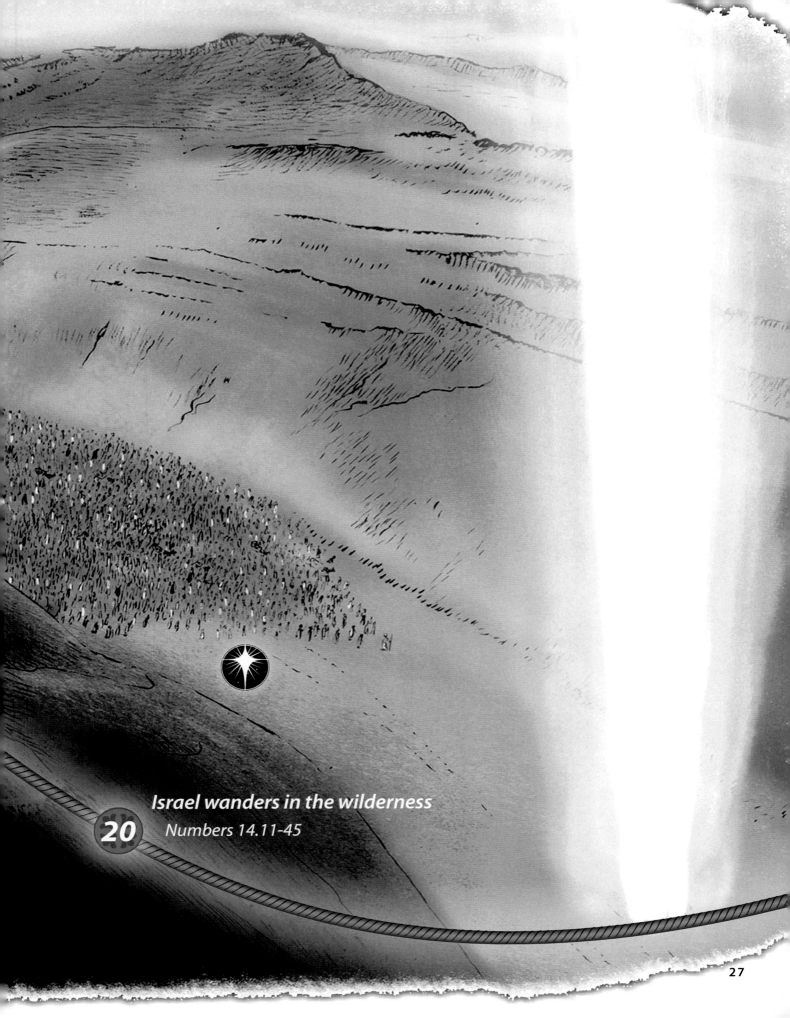

Israel wanders in the wilderness
20 *Numbers 14.11-45*

The priests carry the Ark into the Jordan River

Joshua 3-4

22 *Joshua leads the victory over Jericho*

Joshua 5.13-6.27

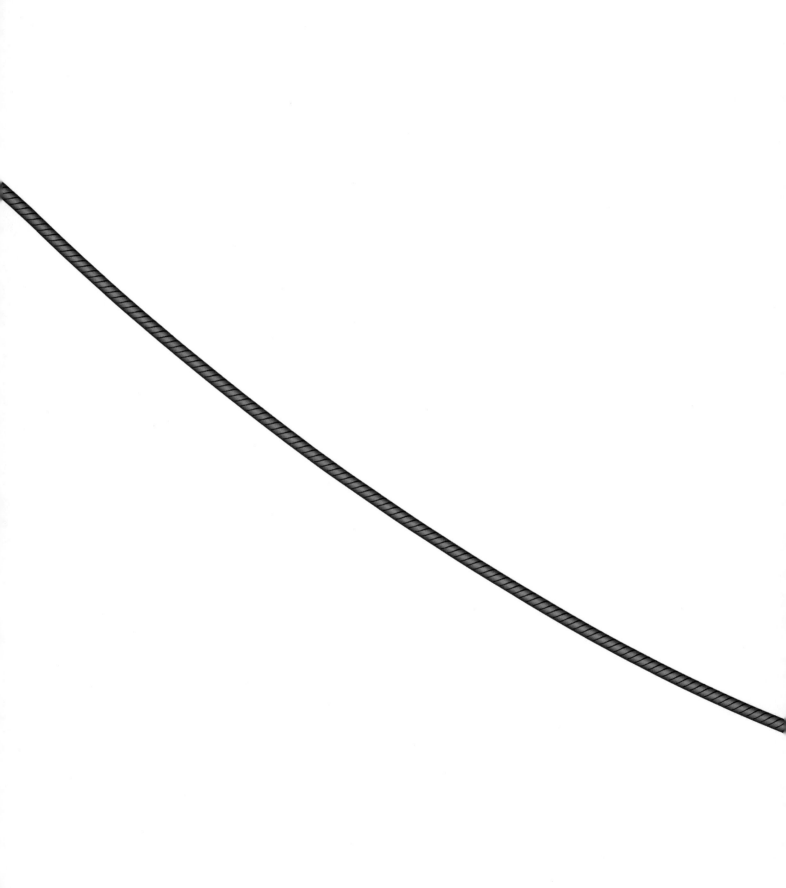

The Promised Land

Gideon asks the Lord for a sign
Judges 6-7

24 **Samson brings down the walls on the Philistines**
Judges 16

Samuel proclaims Saul king **25**
1 Samuel 10.19

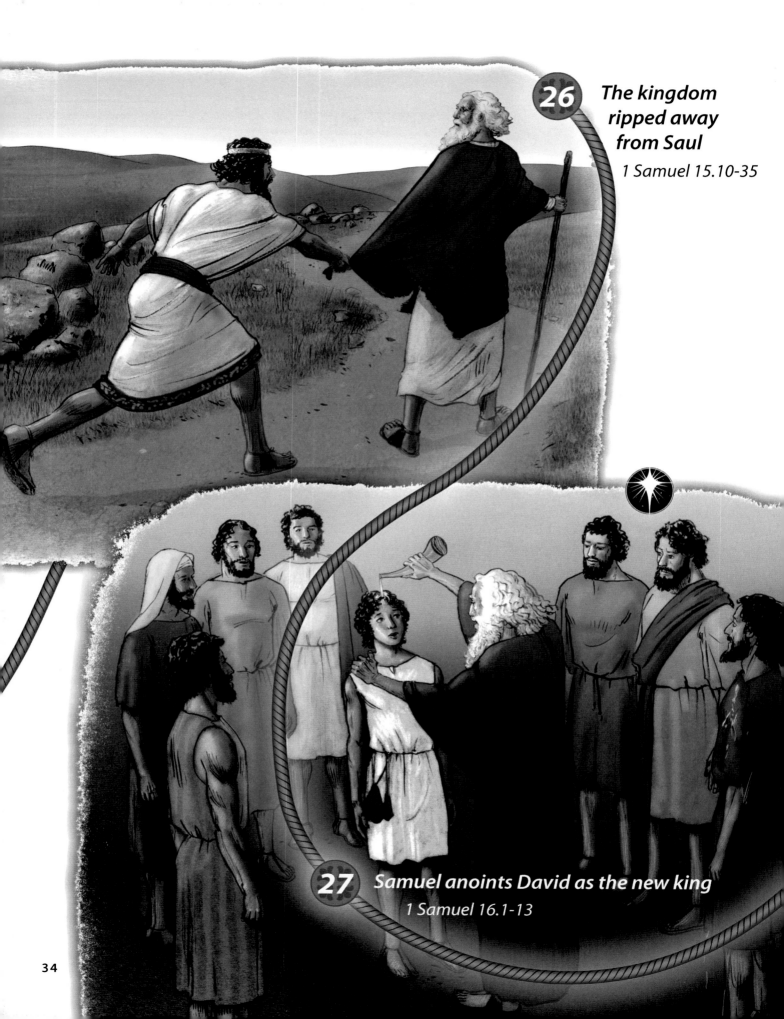

26 **The kingdom ripped away from Saul**
1 Samuel 15.10-35

27 **Samuel anoints David as the new king**
1 Samuel 16.1-13

28 *David fights the giant Goliath*
1 Samuel 17

29 **Solomon gives a wise judgment**
1 Kings 3

Solomon's temple for the Lord
1 Kings 8

30

36

The Exile

Elijah calls down fire from heaven
1 Kings 18.1-40

31

32 *The Lord opens the eyes of Elisha's servant*
2 Kings 6.8-23

33 *Jonah is thrown overboard*

Jonah 1-4

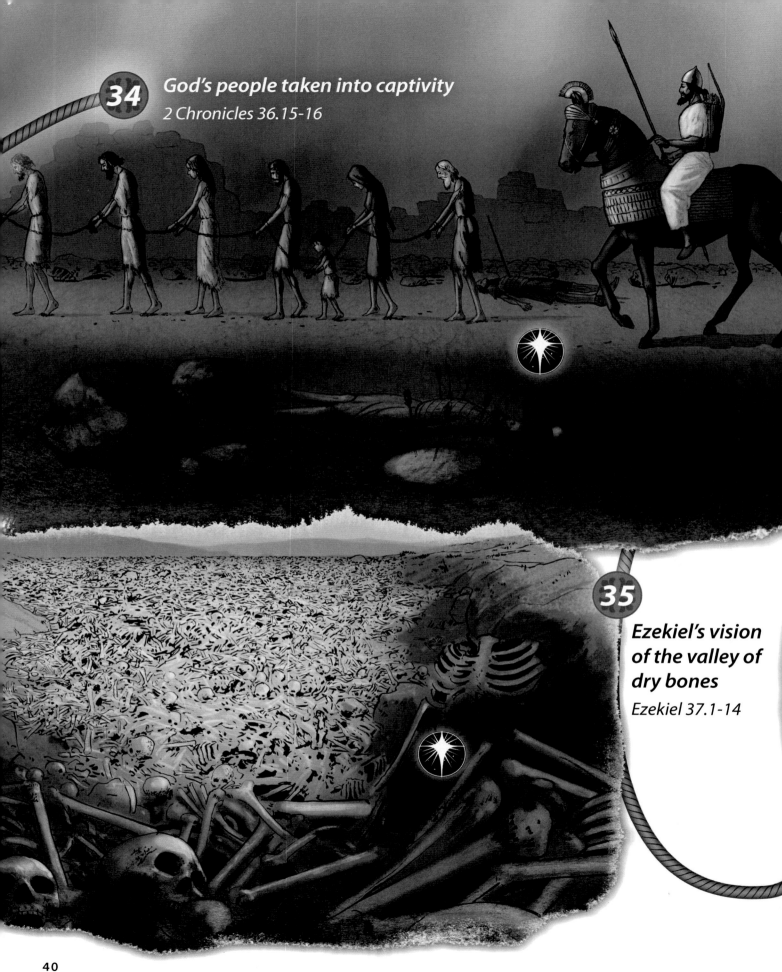

34 *God's people taken into captivity*
2 Chronicles 36.15-16

35

Ezekiel's vision of the valley of dry bones
Ezekiel 37.1-14

The three Hebrew boys in the fiery furnace

Daniel 3

36

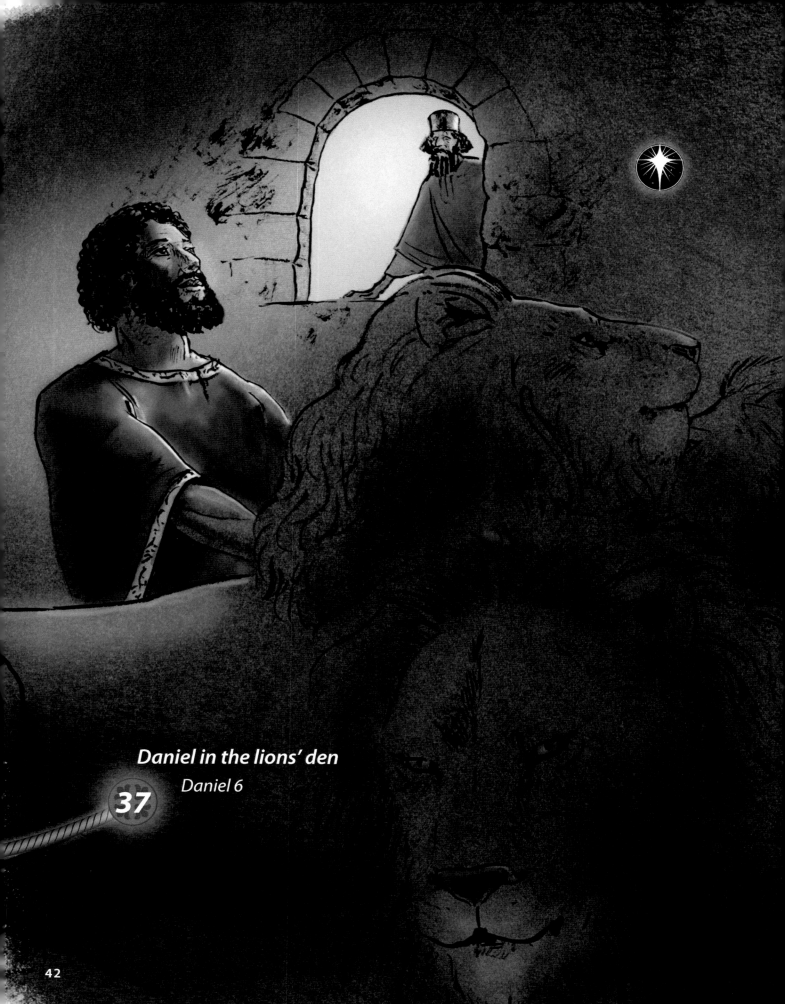

Daniel in the lions' den
Daniel 6

37

The Remnant of Israel

Rebuilding the Temple 38
Ezra 3-6

Rebuilding the walls of Jerusalem 39
Nehemiah 1-8

Ezra reads God's Law to the people
Nehemiah 8

40 *Esther approaches the king of Persia*
Esther 3-8

41 *"Thus says the Lord . . ."*
Isaiah 11.1-9

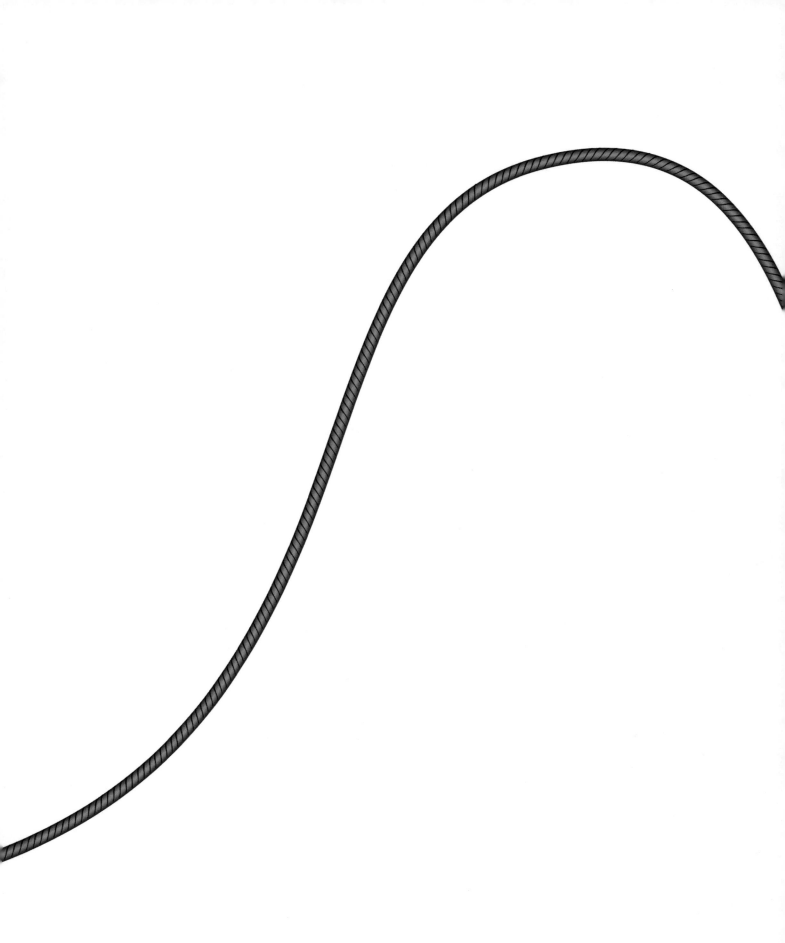

The Story of God in Christ

The Fullness of Time

Advent

Christmas

Epiphany

Lent

Holy Week

The Resurrection of Christ

The Ascension of Christ

Pentecost

Kingdomtide

Advent

···

The Coming of Christ

Advent joyously affirms the First and Second Comings of our Lord.
Through the prophets, God foretold the Messiah's appearing to his people, Israel.
Through the angels, he announced his birth to Zechariah, Mary, and the shepherds.
Let us reverently ponder the sure promise of God – the Deliverer will come
and ransom captive Israel and the world.

The Promise to
Adam and Eve
Genesis 3.15

The Promise
to Abraham
Genesis 12.1-3; 15.5

The Covenant
with David
2 Samuel 7.11-16

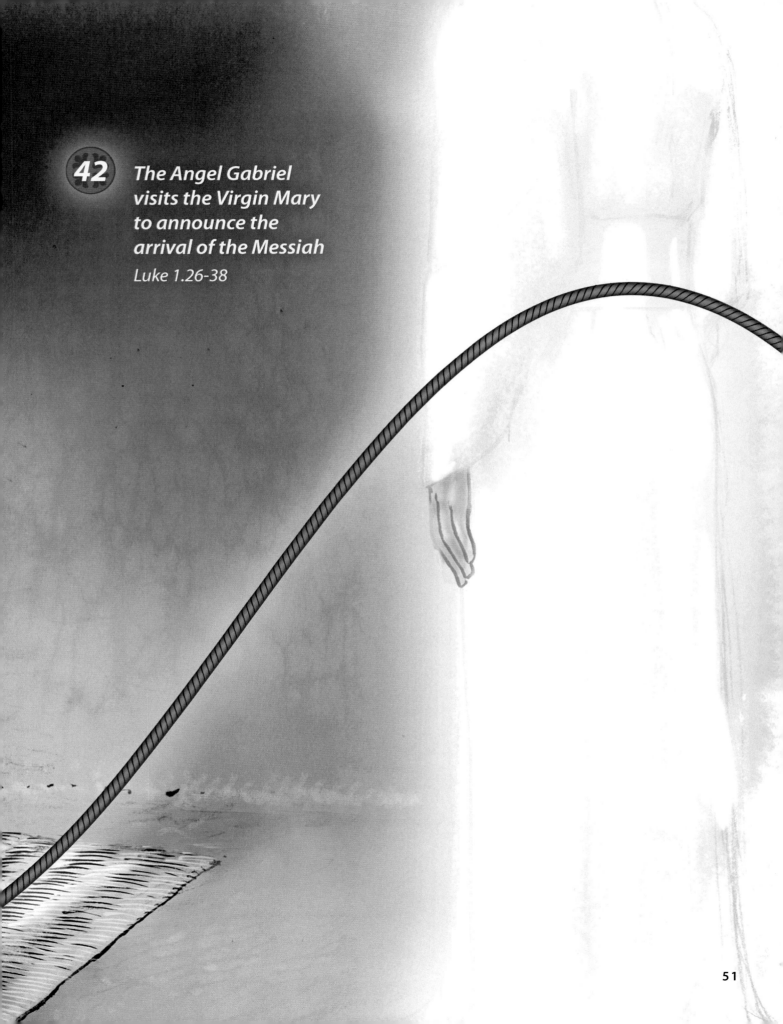

42 *The Angel Gabriel visits the Virgin Mary to announce the arrival of the Messiah*

Luke 1.26-38

43 Elizabeth receives Mary,
the mother of the Messiah

Luke 1.39-56

Lot fleeing
God's wrath
Genesis 19

Whose side
are you on?
Joshua 5.13-15

44

John the Baptist
prepares the way for Messiah
Matthew 3.1-12

53

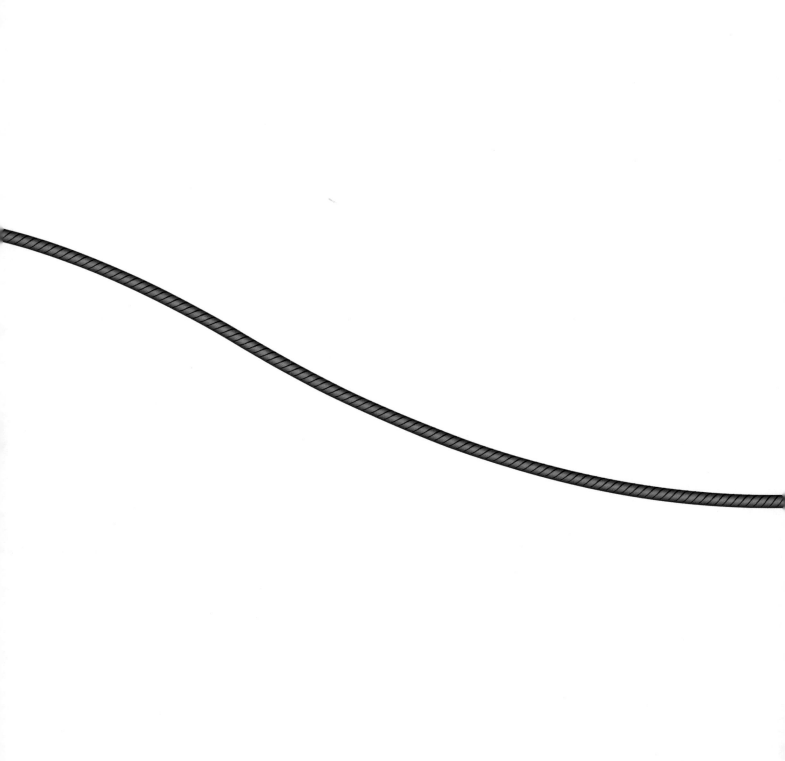

Christmas

The Birth of Christ

Christmas celebrates the birth of Messiah, Jesus,
who is the incarnation of the Son of God, Mary's child.
He is the Word made flesh, the conqueror who enters this fallen world
to reveal to us the Father's love, to destroy the devil's work,
and to redeem his people from their sins.

45 Mary and Joseph journey to Bethlehem
Luke 2.1-5

The Lord spoke through the prophets
Micah 5.2

Christic is born in Bethlehem! **46**
Matthew 1.18-25;
Luke 2.6-7

47

The angels announce the birth of Jesus to the shepherds

Luke 2.8-20

48 Simeon takes Jesus in his arms and praises God

Luke 2.22-39

The Lord gives the Law
Exodus 34.29-35

The prophetess Anna praises God and tells others about Jesus

Luke 2.36-39

Epiphany

··

The Manifestation of Christ

Epiphany commemorates the coming of the Magi,
the wise men from the East who followed the star in search of the Christ child.
This season emphasizes Christ's mission to and for the world.
The light of God's salvation is revealed to all peoples
in the person of Jesus, the Son of God.

The Magi give gifts to Jesus

49

Matthew 2.1-12

John baptizes Jesus in the Jordan River

Matthew 3.13-17

50

Noah's ark
Genesis 6-9

The Red Sea
Exodus 14-15

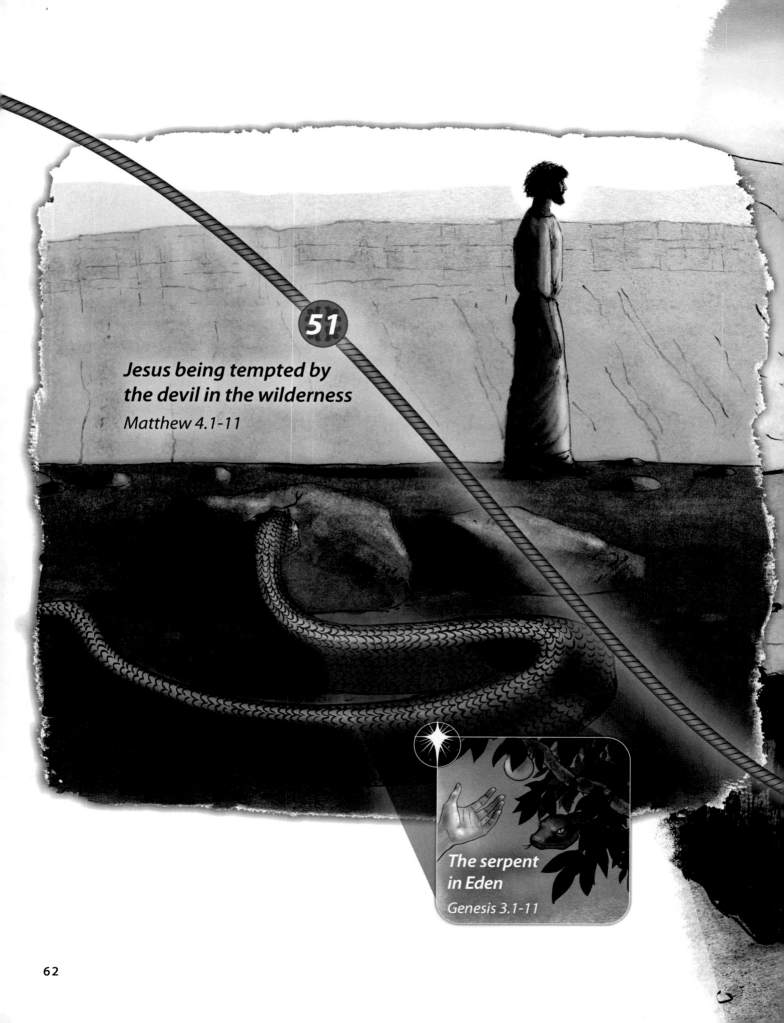

51

Jesus being tempted by the devil in the wilderness

Matthew 4.1-11

The serpent in Eden

Genesis 3.1-11

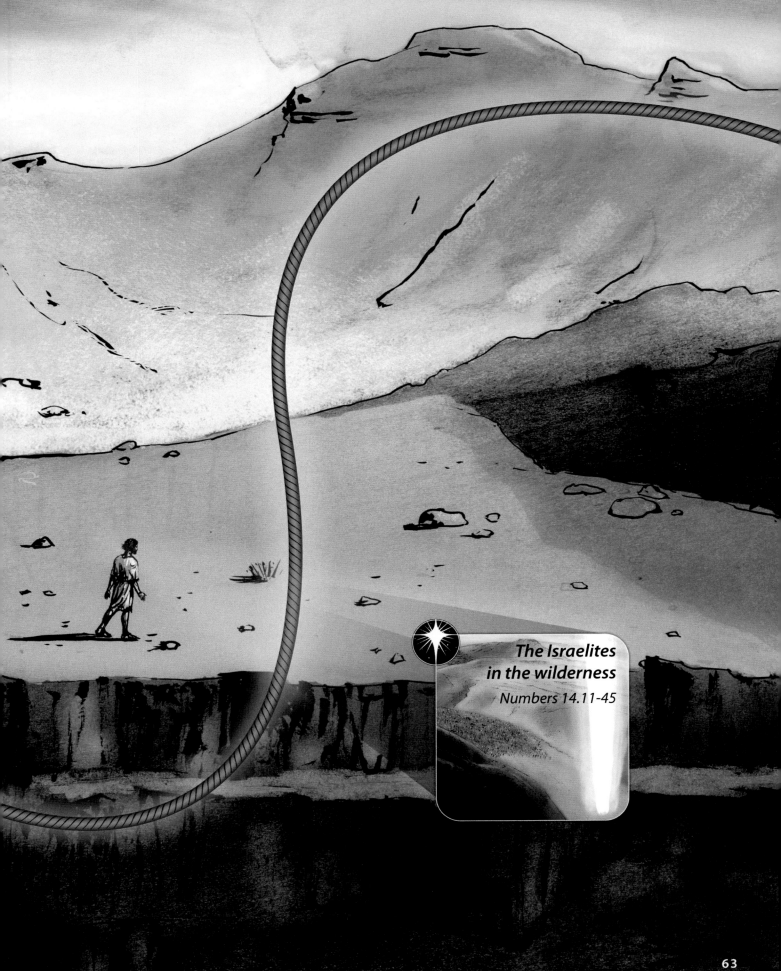

The Israelites
in the wilderness
Numbers 14.11-45

Jesus calls his first disciples 52

Matthew 4.18-22

The Promise to Abraham

Genesis 12,15

53

Jesus feeds 5,000 with a little boy's lunch

John 6.1-15

Jesus heals the Gerasene demoniac
Mark 5.1-20

54

Jesus heals Jairus's daughter
55
Mark 5.21-24, 35-43

A woman healed after twelve years of hemorrhaging
56
Mark 5.25-34

The parable of the sower and the soils

Matthew 13.1-8, 18-23

57

58 *Jesus compares the Kingdom of God to a mustard bush*

Matthew 13.31-32

59 Jesus walks on the water
Matthew 14.22-33

60 The transfiguration of Christ
Matthew 17.1-8

Moses's shining face
Exodus 34.29

Lent

···

The Lowliness of Christ

*The Lenten Season, a forty-day period
starting on Ash Wednesday and ending on Holy Saturday of Holy Week,
calls us to reflect on Jesus's suffering, crucifixion, and death.
As disciples of the humble Nazarene, we embrace his lowliness and humility,
seeking to share the mind of him who was obedient to death,
even death on a cross.*

"Get behind me, Satan!"

Mark 8.27-9.1

61

62 *Jesus tells a parable of a man who is beaten and left for dead*

Luke 10.25-37

A Levite avoids the man

Luke 10.25-37

The Samaritan helps the man

Luke 10.25-37

**The shepherd leaves
the ninety-nine to
find the one lost sheep**

Luke 15.1-7

63

64

The parable of the prodigal son; the son leaves the father

Luke 15.11-32

The son returns
Luke 15.11-32

Jesus calls to Zacchaeus

65

Luke 19.1-10

66 *Jesus on the road going up to Jerusalem*

Mark 10.32-45

Holy Week

· ·

The Passion of Christ

Holy Week recalls the events of our Lord's suffering and death.
We recall his triumphant entry into Jerusalem on Palm Sunday,
his giving of the commandments on Maundy Thursday,
his crucifixion and burial on Good Friday,
and the solemn vigil of Saturday night before Easter Sunday.

68

Jesus shares a final
Passover meal with the disciples

Luke 22.7-23

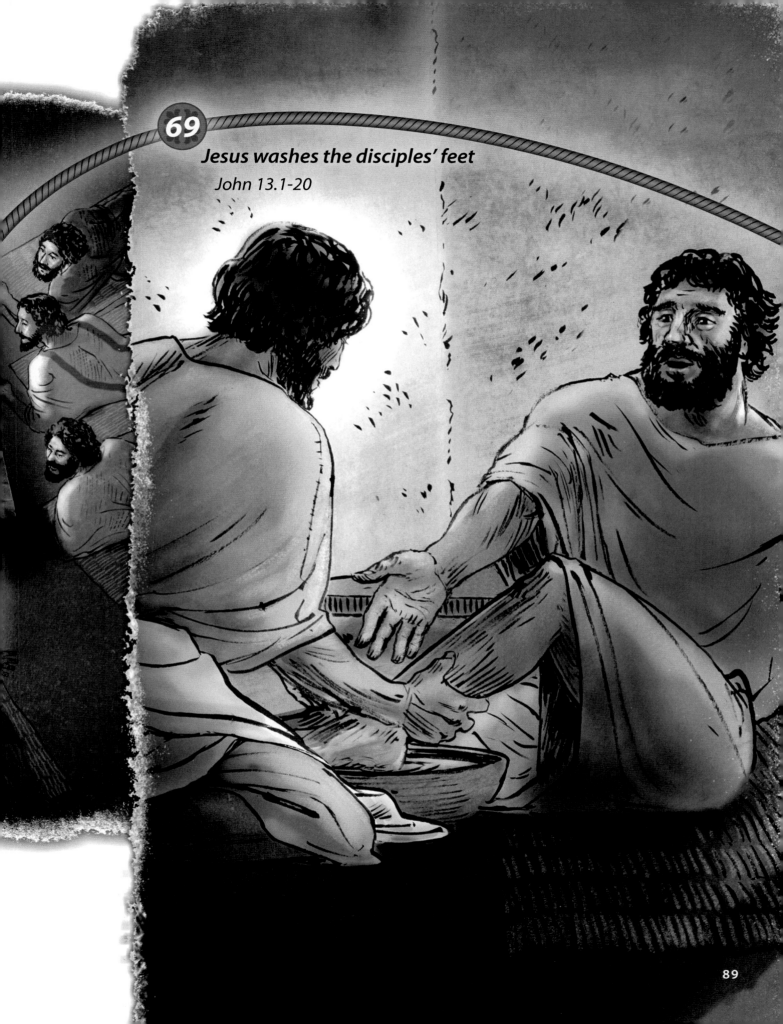

69

Jesus washes the disciples' feet
John 13.1-20

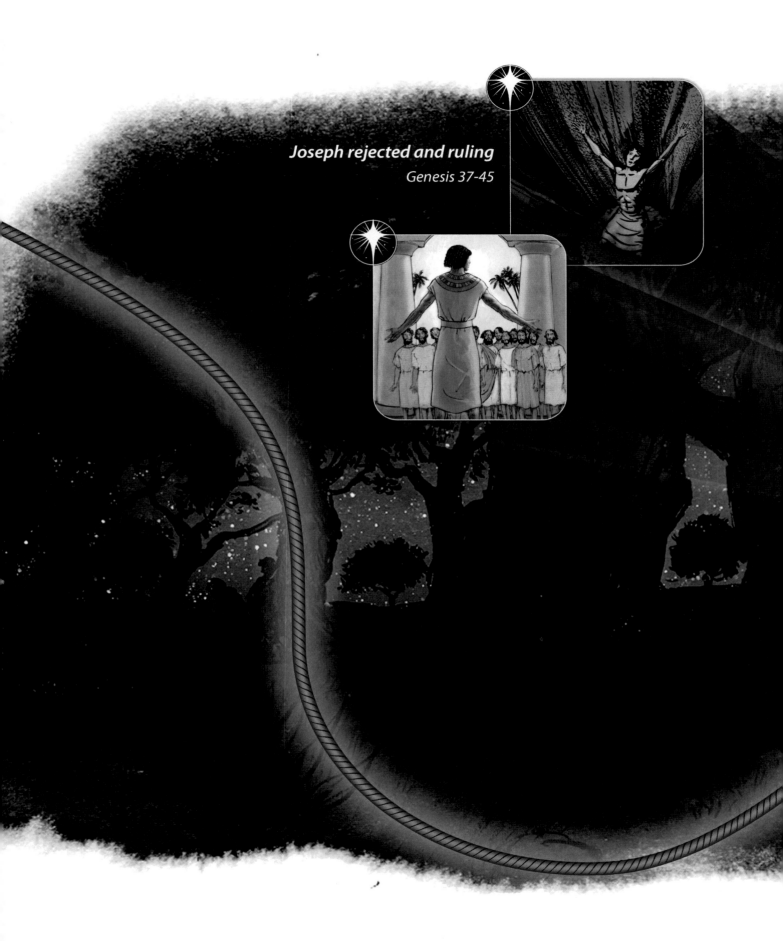

Joseph rejected and ruling
Genesis 37-45

70

Jesus prays in the Garden of Gethsemane

Matthew 26.36-46

71

*Judas betrays
Jesus with a kiss*

Matthew 22.47-56

72

**The Jews convince
Pilate to have Jesus killed**

John 18.28-19.16

Pilate has
Jesus flogged

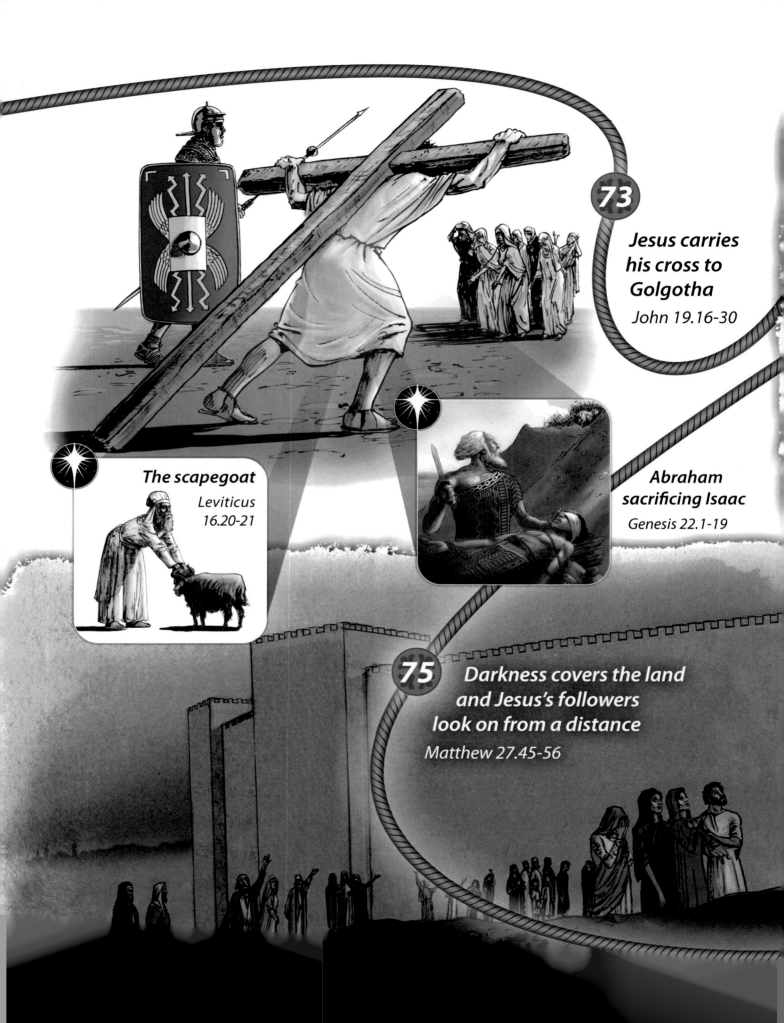

73

Jesus carries his cross to Golgotha

John 19.16-30

The scapegoat

Leviticus 16.20-21

Abraham sacrificing Isaac

Genesis 22.1-19

75

Darkness covers the land and Jesus's followers look on from a distance

Matthew 27.45-56

74 *Jesus is crucified between two criminals*
Luke 23.32-43

The bronze serpent
Numbers 21.4-9

The lamb on the altar
Deuteronomy 16.1-8

The blood on the doorposts
Exodus 12.7-13

76

Joseph of Arimathea and Nicodemus prepare to put Jesus in a tomb

John 19.38-42

Eastertide

The Resurrection of Christ

On Easter Sunday we celebrate the bodily resurrection of Jesus.
The same lowly Nazarene – he who was betrayed by his own disciple,
who suffered under Pilate's cruel gaze, who was crucified
on a Roman cross, and who was buried in a borrowed tomb –
the same Lord rose triumphantly on the third day.
Jesus has risen from death to life through the power of God.
"Christ is risen! He is risen, indeed!"

Guarding Jesus's tomb

Matthew 27.62-66

Israel taken into exile
2 Chronicles 36.15-18

Jonah swallowed by a fish
Jonah 1-4

Terrified guards flee the tomb

Matthew 28.1-4

78

79 *Three women come to Jesus's tomb and find it open and empty*

Luke 24.1-12

80

*Jesus appears to
Mary Magdalene*

John 20.11-18

81

After his resurrection, Jesus appears to his disciples

Luke 24.36-49

Eastertide

The Ascension of Christ

*For forty days after his resurrection, Jesus revealed himself alive to his disciples.
On the fortieth day, he ascended to heaven to take his place
as Lord and Christ at God's right hand.
Ten days after this, on the fiftieth day after his resurrection,
he would send to us the promise of the Father –
the Holy Spirit, the pledge of our salvation.
Here we ponder the wonder of God's working,
from Easter Sunday to the Spirit's descent at Pentecost.*

"Go therefore, and make disciples of all nations . . ."
Matthew 28.16-20

82

Elijah taken into heaven

2 Kings 2

Melchizedek

Genesis 14.17-24

83

Jesus ascends to the right hand of the Father

Acts 1.6-11

Pentecost

. . . .

The Coming of the Holy Spirit

*On Pentecost we commemorate the descent of the Holy Spirit to earth
on Christ's believers, his infilling of the people of God, the Church.
Through him, the third person of the Trinity,
Jesus our Lord is now present with his people.
The Spirit is the guarantee of the promised inheritance to come.
We ponder the fullness and mystery of our God's person and work
in our celebration on Trinity Sunday.*

The Holy Spirit comes on the believers at Pentecost

Acts 2.1-47

84

The valley of the dry bones

Ezekiel 37.1-14

The Lord spoke through the prophets

Joel 2.28-32

85 Paul shares the testimony of his conversion and calling

Acts 22.1-21

Kingdomtide

The Last Times: The Story Continues Today

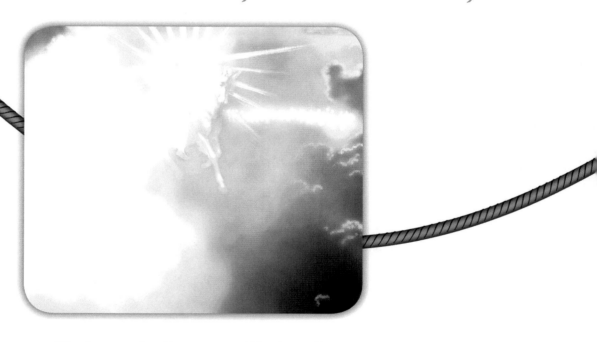

*The Season after Pentecost, or Kingdomtide,
is a season of Christ's headship, harvest, and hope.
As Christus Victor, Jesus is exalted at God's right hand.
He is the head of the body, the Church, and he is Lord of the harvest,
empowering his people to bear witness of his saving grace in the world
and gather the harvest of souls so ripe for reaping.
Likewise, this is a season of the blessed hope, as we look to
Christ's sure return to complete God's salvation for the world.*

The Apostle Paul imprisoned for his Gospel testimony

Acts 16.16-34

86

Daniel in the lions' den

2 Timothy 4.16

*Repentance and forgiveness
of sins in the name of Jesus
proclaimed to all nations*

Acts 10.34-43

87

Christian Martyrs
(Rome, first to fourth centuries)

Sharing in his suffering and death
(Philippians 3.10)

Augustine of Hippo
(North Africa, fourth to fifth century)

Transformed by the renewing of the mind
(Romans 12.2)

St. Francis of Assisi
(Italy, twelfth to thirteenth century)

Preach the Gospel to all creation
(Mark 16.15)

Martin Luther
(Germany, fifteenth to sixteenth century)

Not ashamed
of the Gospel
(Romans 1.16)

*Christ is ransoming
for God saints from
every tribe and language
and people and nation*
Revelation 5

EDMOND BETTUS BRIDGE

Martin Luther King, Jr.
(United States of America, twentieth century)

Let justice roll down (Amos 5.24)

**Mother Teresa
of Calcutta**
(India, twentieth century)

To the least of these
(Matthew 25.40)

89

Christ will come again and destroy death and the devil forever

Revelation 19

90 *A new heaven and a new earth*
Revelation 21.3-4

. . . and the Story will never end . . .

Made in the USA
Columbia, SC
04 February 2021